How to Dress a Po' Boy

How to Dress a Po' Boy

Written and Illustrated by
Johnette Downing

PELICAN PUBLISHING COMPANY
Gretna 2013

In memory of Dr. Milburn Calhoun

The word "Pelican" and the depiction of a pelican are trademarks of Pelican Publishing Company, Inc., and are registered in the U.S. Patent and Trademark Office.

Library of Congress Cataloging-in-Publication Data

Downing, Johnette.
 How to dress a po' boy / written and Illustrated by Johnette Downing.
   pages cm
 ISBN 978-1-4556-1719-7 (hardcover : alk. paper) —
ISBN 978-1-4556-1720-3 (e-book) 1. Sandwiches—Juvenile literature. 2. Cooking, American—Louisiana style—Juvenile literature. I. Title.
       TX818.D69 2013
        641.84—dc23

                          2012028430

Special thanks to poorboyologist Michael Mizell-Nelson, Chef John Folse, and Parkway Bakery for serving me loaves of information "dressed" as I researched the book, to Reily Foods Company for generously granting permission to use Blue Plate® Mayonnaise in the book, to Elizabeth Adams, to my foodie Michael Sartisky, to my photographer Thom Bennett, and to the Pelican Publishing family for believing in my work.

Printed in Malaysia
Published by Pelican Publishing Company, Inc.
1000 Burmaster Street, Gretna, Louisiana 70053

HOW TO DRESS A PO' BOY

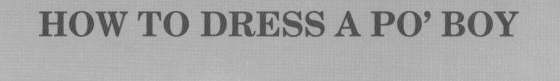

A po' boy is a sandwich,
as everybody knows.
"Dressed" is with all the fixings,
and this is how it goes.

First you start with bread,
long French bread.

Then you add mayonnaise,
Blue Plate® Mayonnaise.

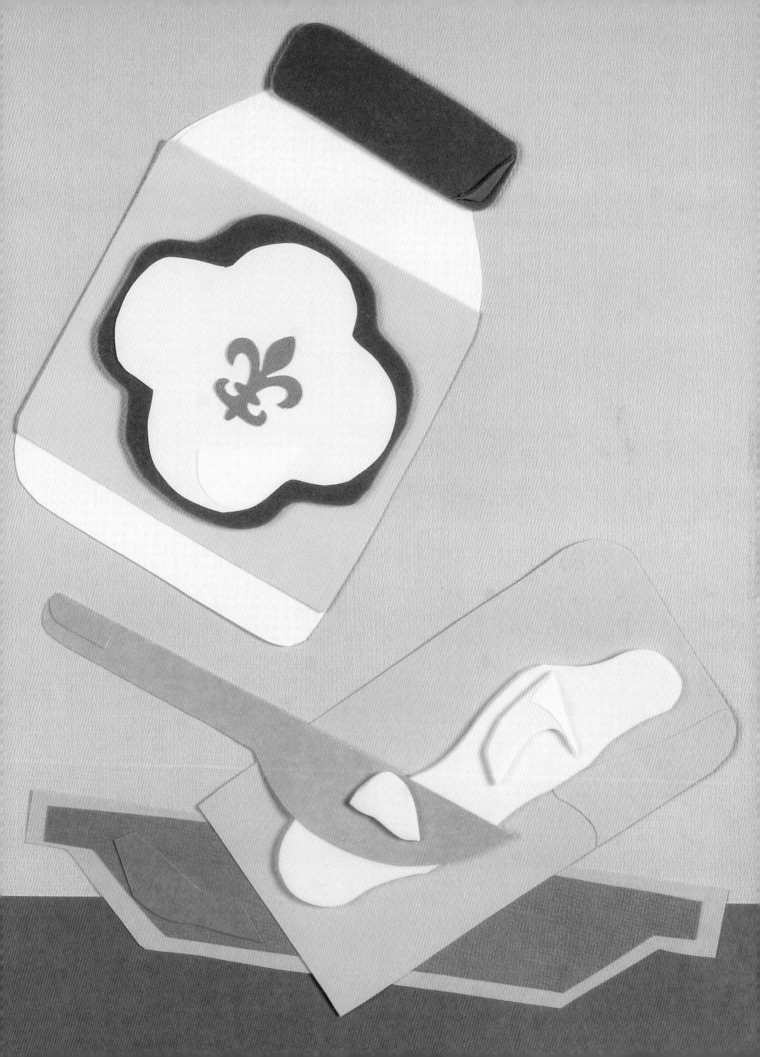

Come on now,
we are learning how
to dress a po' boy.
Girl or boy, let's all enjoy
a Louisiana po' boy.

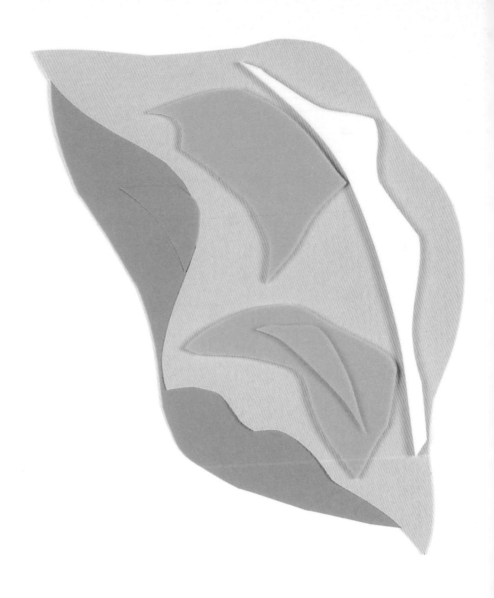

Lay down a bed of lettuce,
leafy green lettuce.

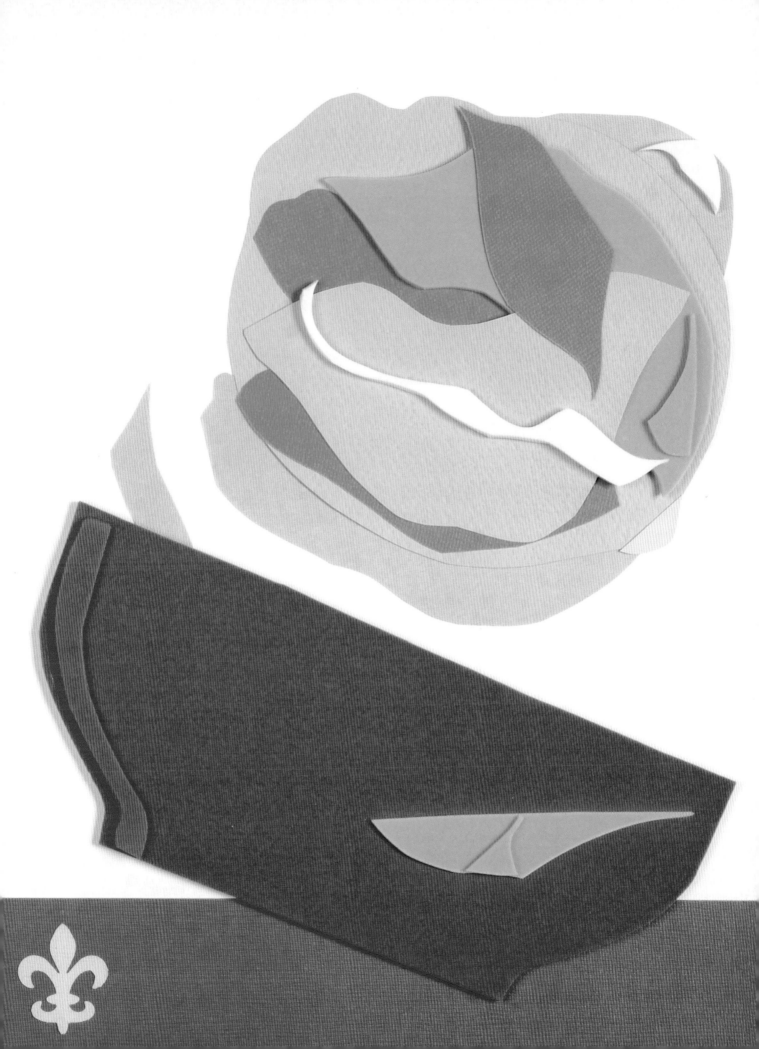

Follow with tomato,
sliced Creole tomato.

Perk it up with pickles,
sliced dill pickles.

Spice it up with hot sauce,
Louisiana hot sauce.

Come on now,
we are learning how
to dress a po' boy.
Girl or boy, let's all enjoy
a Louisiana po' boy.

Top it off with meat,
any kind of meat:
shrimp, catfish,
soft-shell crab,
roast beef, debris . . .

Italian meatballs, crawfish,
sausage, or alligator.

Come on now,
we are learning how
to dress a po' boy.
Girl or boy, let's all enjoy
a Louisiana po' boy.

Then you put them all together,
yeah you right.
Now your po' boy is dressed.
Take a bite.

Ooooweeee!

Come on now, we learned how
to dress a po' boy.
Girl or boy, let's all enjoy
a Louisiana po' boy.

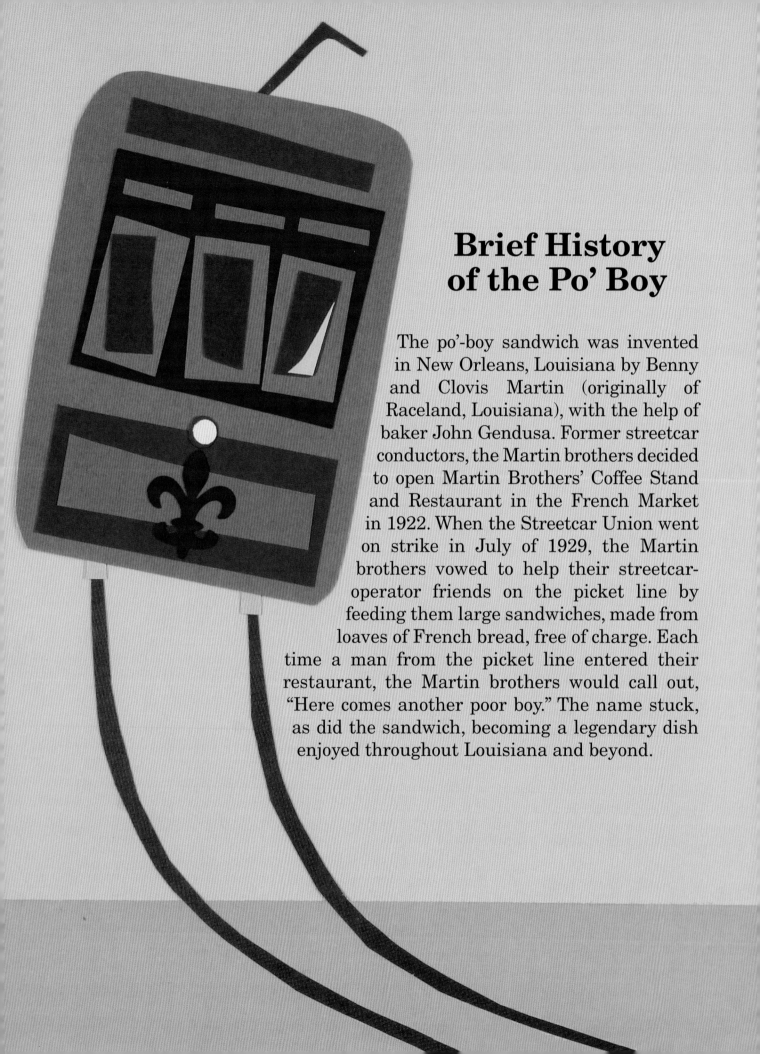

Brief History of the Po' Boy

The po'-boy sandwich was invented in New Orleans, Louisiana by Benny and Clovis Martin (originally of Raceland, Louisiana), with the help of baker John Gendusa. Former streetcar conductors, the Martin brothers decided to open Martin Brothers' Coffee Stand and Restaurant in the French Market in 1922. When the Streetcar Union went on strike in July of 1929, the Martin brothers vowed to help their streetcar-operator friends on the picket line by feeding them large sandwiches, made from loaves of French bread, free of charge. Each time a man from the picket line entered their restaurant, the Martin brothers would call out, "Here comes another poor boy." The name stuck, as did the sandwich, becoming a legendary dish enjoyed throughout Louisiana and beyond.

Word Menu

Blue Plate® Mayonnaise
Originating in New Orleans in 1927, this condiment is a tradition in households and is used as a key ingredient on any po' boy. It's in my refrigerator right now! It's a staple, like bread and water.

Creole tomato
You haven't eaten a tomato until you've eaten a Creole tomato; no, really! It is so beloved that the Creole tomato, though technically a fruit, was designated as the official vegetable plant of Louisiana in 2003. This hearty, deep-red, bold tomato loves the hot, humid weather and rich river soil found in Southeast Louisiana. What wouldn't?

Debris
No, this is not trash or something to throw out. Debris is the yummy drippings and pieces of meat scraped off the bottom of the pan after you've cooked roast beef. It's where all the seasoning lands, so you know it's going be good. Slap a spoonful of debris on French bread and you have yourself a unique po' boy!

Dressed
"Do you want it dressed?" is one of the first questions you will be asked after ordering a po' boy. Don't worry, you are not being asked about fashion. You are being asked if you want lettuce, tomato, pickles, and mayonnaise on your sandwich. Whatever you do, don't say you want it "undressed." That's just silly!

French bread
At the risk of sounding boastful, Louisiana French bread is like no other. Bread by any other name can smell as sweet, but it won't be as light, airy, crispy, and flaky as Louisiana French bread. Without Louisiana French bread, it's not a po' boy. Period!

Hot sauce
If you think the weather in Louisiana is hot, wait until you try our state's variety of hot sauces. A favorite on a New Orleans po' boy, this spicy condiment puts the "hot" in "hot sauce," no lie!

Po' boy
This delicious Louisiana original sandwich is made with French bread, lettuce, tomato, pickles, mayonnaise, and your choice of meat, typically fried seafood (oysters, shrimp, catfish, soft-shell crab, crawfish, or a combination of these), roast beef and gravy, hot sausage, meatballs, ham, or just about anything you can imagine. Spread on a little Creole mustard as *lagniappe* (something extra), to make this Louisiana sandwich one you'll never forget. Yeah you right!

How to Dress a Po' Boy

By Johnette Downing
© 2011 Johnette Downing, Wiggle Worm Records Publishing ASCAP

A po' boy is a sand - wich___ as ev - 'ry - bod - y knows.

"Dressed" with all the fix-ings___ and this is how it goes. First you start with bread,

long French bread. Then you add the may-on-naise,___ Blue Plate® May - on - naise.

Come on now, we're learn - ing how___ to dress a po' boy.

Girl or boy, let's all en - joy___ a Lou - is - i - a - na___ po' boy.